1

Jochen Rindt World Champion F1 Driver

by
Bill Rosoman

Copyright 2012 Bill Rosoman

ISBN 978-1-927157-34-3

Table of Contents

About the Author

I have lived an interesting and varied life. Currently I am unemployed and living in a Mobile Home (RV) mostly at a property I have purchased out the back country. Life is full of surprises and chances.

I really regret little in my life, of cause if I had my life over again there are things that I would change. But hey life goes on and follows it's path.

This is our online business card. Just scan with your smart phone or computer to see the card.

Www.creativekiwis.com

I am currently publishing and writing some more ebooks. This is interesting and fun. I am also making some money!

https://www.smashwords.com/profile/view/leftfieldnz

http://goo.gl/MLSLL

I have worked with technology for many years and have been quite prophetic over the years. I have been working on Books and Ebooks online for many years now. It is starting to pay some dividends and we are starting to get some rewards.

I consider myself an Optimistic Realist.

"Optimism has a Chance
Persimmon has no Chance.

Life has had its ups and downs, but general my life has been and is great.

My glass is always half full.

Disclaimer

I have taken care to identify people and web pages I have accessed or used. I acknowledge all copyrights and trademarks.

Introduction

Jochen Rindt is my personal hero and sports hero. I admired his racing style and his presence.

For me he was a brilliant driver and had a great driving style and nerves of steel. I remember seeing him racing vividly.

It was a great tragedy that he died while racing.

In my teenage years of the 1960s I with friends used to attend Motor Racing events, mostly at Levin in New Zealand. There we would watch Motor Racing and really enjoyed it.

I have some photos of the occasions I used to attend. I remember very well Dennis Hulme and drivers like Jochen Rindt.

F1 in the 1960s

In the 1960s there were many accidents as the vehicle designs and the health and safety requirements were not that great.

It was an exciting time and the fact that F1 was held in small countries like New Zealand and that you could be real close to the track and see the action at close quarters was fantastic.

Nowadays little countries like New Zealand do not get a look in on international events. We have had for a few years the Hamilton NZ V8 races. But these stopped this year due to the cost of running the event and the losses incurred.

We do have a local Stock Course near were I live and there are regular Midget Car racing not that far from me either.

I must make the effort to attend some of these events.

I would sincerely love to see a modern F1 race, but sadly I invested what money I had in buying a property and hopefully building a house.

Still seeing a F1 race is top of my Bucket List as they say!

About Jochen Rindt

IMHO Jochen Rindt is the best F1 Driver of all times

He Died and was awarded the F1 World Champion Trophy

posthumously.

F1 is good for entertainment, research, testing new technologies, promotion of products and brands, great fun.

Jochen's death was extremely sad and a very sobering moment for me. The accident did not seem that bad (you can see it on youtube). But he failed to survive the crash against the wall.

F1 Today

I still have a great interest in Motor Racing and F1, but do not get to see very much due to the expense and that it is mostly on pay TV in New Zealand. Added to that I live in a rural community with solar power and do not watch TV.

I do not agree the way sport is run now, it is mostly on pay TV, it is very expensive to attend live events (nearest F1 for me is Australia in March), and it is about money and greed.

Still life would not be the same for me if there were not some things like F1 I could not enjoy now and then.

May Jochen Rindt rest in peace.

Jochen Rindt

From Wikipedia, the free encyclopedia

Born 18 April 1942

Died 5 September 1970 (aged 28)

Formula One World Championship career

Nationality Austrian

Active years 1964 - 1970

Teams Brabham-BRM, Cooper-Climax, Cooper-Maserati, Brabham-Repco, Lotus-Ford

Races 62 (60 starts)

Championships 1 (1970)

Win 6

Podiums 13

Career points 107 (109)[1]

Pole positions 10

Fastest laps 3

First race 1964 Austrian Grand Prix

First win 1969 United States Grand Prix

Last win 1970 German Grand Prix

Last race 1970 Italian Grand Prix

24 Hours of Le Mans career

Participating years 1964 - 1967

Teams NART

Comstock Racing

Porsche

Best finish 1st (1965)

Class wins 1 (1965)

Karl Jochen Rindt (April 18, 1942 Mainz, Germany - September 5, 1970 Monza, Italy) was a German racing driver who represented Austria during his career.[2] He is the only driver to posthumously win the Formula One World Drivers' Championship (in 1970), after being killed in practice for the Italian Grand Prix. Away from Formula One, Rindt was highly successful in other single-seater formulae, as well as sports car racing. In 1965 he won the 24 Hours of Le Mans race, driving a Ferrari 250LM in partnership with Masten Gregory from the United States of America. He was a close friend to Jackie Stewart, and was a neighbour to the Scotsman in Switzerland.

Biography

Jochen Rindt was born in Mainz, Germany, but after his parents were killed in a bombing raid in Hamburg during the Second World War,[3] he was raised by his grandparents in Graz, Austria, where he grew up and started motor racing. Although Rindt never became an Austrian citizen, he did drive his entire career under an Austrian racing licence.[4]

Despite being very successful in Formula 2 (by winning for instance the 1964 London Trophy), Rindt kept on choosing the wrong F1 cars. Rindt made his Formula One début for the Rob Walker Racing Team in the 1964 Austrian Grand Prix. It was to be his only Grand Prix of the year. From 1965 to 1967, Rindt raced for the Cooper Car Company, scoring 32 points in 29 races. In 1968, Rindt raced for Brabham, but his season wasn't what he had hoped for because of technical problems. He also raced in the Indianapolis 500 in both 1967 and 1968, but finished no better than 24th.

Rindt was noted for being an exceptionally fast driver with superb car control and reflexes, but rarely had a car equal to his talent until 1969 when he moved to Lotus and his career took off. Rindt clinched the first Grand Prix victory of his career in the 1969 Grand Prix of the USA in Watkins Glen. Rindt finished that year with 22 points, giving him fourth place in the Formula 1 World Championship. Rindt occasionally had a fraught relationship with Colin Chapman as he preferred a stable technological footing as opposed to Chapman's need to innovate and invent, but the two forged a successful partnership. Rindt's first victory in the 1970 season was at Monaco, where he overtook Jack Brabham in the last corner. With the Lotus 72, Rindt won four more Grands Prix in The Netherlands, France, Britain and Germany that year.

During practice for the 1970 Italian Grand Prix in Monza, near Milan, Chapman and Rindt agreed to follow the lead of Jackie Stewart (Tyrrell) and Denny Hulme (McLaren) and run without wings in an attempt to reduce drag and gain a higher top speed. The more powerful Flat-12 Ferraris of Jacky Ickx and Clay Regazzoni had been up to 10 mph (16 km/h) faster than the Lotus at the previous race in Austria. Rindt's team mate John Miles was unhappy with the wingless setup in Friday practice, reporting that the car "wouldn't run straight". Rindt reported no such problems, and Chapman recalled that Rindt reported the car to be "almost 800 rpm faster on the straight" without wings.[5]

On the following day, Rindt ran with higher gear ratios fitted to his car to take advantage of the reduced drag, increasing the car's potential top speed to 205 mph (330 km/h).[6] On Rindt's fifth lap of the final practice session, Hulme, who was following, reported that under braking for the Parabolica corner: "Jochen's car weaved slightly and then swerved sharp left into the crash barrier."[7] A joint in the crash barrier parted, the suspension dug in under the barrier, and the car hit a stanchion head on. The front end of the car was destroyed. Although the 28 year old Rindt was rushed to hospital, he was pronounced dead. Rindt had only recently acquiesced to not wearing the crotch straps, as he wanted to be able to get out of the car fast in case of fire, he was however wearing his shoulder straps, this according to his mechanic Herbie Blash in an interview on a documentary on ORF1 Television (aired 5 September 2010). He was the second Lotus team leader to be killed in two years, as Jim Clark had been killed in 1968 in a Formula 2 race at Hockenheim. An Italian court later found that the accident was initiated by a failure of the car's right front brakeshaft, but that Rindt's death was caused by poorly installed crash barriers.[8]

Rindt is buried at the central cemetery (Zentralfriedhof) in Graz.

At the time he died Rindt had won five of that year's ten Grands Prix, which meant that he had a strong lead in the World Championship. At that stage he theoretically could have been overtaken by Ferrari driver Jacky Ickx. However Rindt's Lotus team mate, Emerson Fittipaldi, won the penultimate Grand Prix of the year at Watkins Glen, USA, depriving Ickx of the points he needed to win the title, and so Rindt became motor racing's only posthumous World Champion.[9] The trophy was presented to his Finnish widow Nina Rindt nee Lincoln, daughter of famous Finnish racer, Curt Lincoln. In a tragic twist of irony, it was learned that Jochen had already promised Nina he would retire from F1 if he won the world championship.[10]

http://www.youtube.com/watch?v=Mze8qk7sN2o

http://goo.gl/81Wuz

http://www.jochen-rindt.at/index.html

1970 Jochen Rindt (A) Rindt died in a heavy crash with his Lotus at the parabolica corner in Monza, Italy. Although Rindt was rushed to hospital, he was pronounced dead. That same year he was honoured posthumously with the World Championship title.

List of Formula One fatal accidents

From Wikipedia, the free encyclopedia

http://en.wikipedia.org/wiki/List_of_Formula_One_fatal_accidents

Five drivers have died while driving a Formula One car at the Nürburgring; only the Indianapolis Motor Speedway has had more casualties.

Formula One, abbreviated to F1, is the highest class of open-wheeled auto racing defined by the Fédération Internationale de l'Automobile

(FIA), motorsport's world governing body.[1] The F1 world championship season consists of a series of races, known as Grands Prix, held usually on purpose-built circuits, and in a few cases on closed city streets. The results of each race are combined to determine two annual Championships, one for drivers and one for constructors.

The list consists of all the drivers who have died during a FIA World Championship race weekend, or elsewhere while driving a Formula One car. It does not include track marshals and other race attendees, or F1 races held before the inauguration of the World Championship in 1950. Forty-seven drivers have died in this fashion, twenty-four during a World Championship Grand Prix race weekend, seven during Indianapolis 500 races when it was part of the Formula One World Championship,[nb 1] nine during a test session and six during a non-championship Formula One event.

Fifteen drivers died in the 1950s; fourteen in the 1960s; twelve in the 1970s; four in the 1980s and two in the 1990s. No driver has suffered a fatal accident since 1994, making this the longest period in F1 history without a driver fatality. Drivers from the United Kingdom have suffered the most fatal accidents, 12 in all, the most recent being Tom Pryce in 1977. Only two Formula One Champions have died while racing or practising in Formula One, Jochen Rindt in 1970, and Ayrton Senna in 1994.

http://www.f1complete.com/content/view/228/383/

All Formula 1 deaths

Saturday, 03 September 2005 23:07 Written by Administrator

F1 RECORDS AND STATS: Driver records   Team records   F1 facts History F1 deaths

Name Nation Date Place

(q)=qualifying

Ayrton Senna Brazil May 1, 1994 San Marino GP

Roland Ratzenberger Austria April 30, 1994 San Marino GP(q)

Ricardo Paletti Italy June 13, 1982 Canadian GP

Gilles Villeneuve Canada May 8, 1982 Belgian GP (q)

Ronnie Peterson Sweden Sept. 10, 1978 Italian GP

Tom Pryce Britain May 5, 1977 South African GP

Mark Donahue United States Aug. 19, 1975 Austrian GP (q)

Helmuth Koinigg Austria October 6, 1974 U.S. GP

Francois Cevert France October 7, 1973 U.S. GP (q)

Roger Williamson Britain July 29, 1973 Dutch GP

Jochen Rindt Austria Sept. 5, 1970 Italian GP (q)

Piers Courage Britain June 7, 1970 Dutch GP

Gerhard Mitter West-Germany August 2, 1969 German GP (q)

Jo Schlesser France July 7, 1968 French GP

Lorenzo BandiniItaly May 10, 1967 Monaco GP

John Taylor Britain August 7, 1966 German GP

Carel Godin de Beaufort Netherlands August 2 1964 German GP (q)

Wolfgang Von Trips West-Germany Sept. 10, 1961 Italian GP

Chris Bristow Britain June 19, 1960 Belgian GP

Alan Stacey Britain June 19, 1960 Belgian GP

Stuart Lewis-Evans Britain Sept. 19, 1958 Moroccan GP

Peter Collins Britain August 3, 1958 German GP

Luigi Musso Italy July 6, 1958 French GP

Onofre Marimon Argentina July 31, 1954 German GP (q)

These are some of my racing photos from the 1970s, especially were I saw Jochen Rindt race at the Levin Racing Circuit in New Zealand.

These two are probably at Silverstone Raceway in the UK, I visited there in 1969-70 while on my big OE.

These were great times and I really enjoyed the motor racing.

Conclusion

Jochen Rindt, was a Super F1 driver.

IMHO Jochen Rindt is the best F1 Driver of all times

He Died and was awarded the F1 Trophy posthumously.

Motor Racing in the 1960s and 1970s was an exciting time and the sport was much different than it is today.

Jochen Rindt for me was the pinnacle of a super sportsman and a great person, who lived in times that were much simpler .

Creative Kiwis, an Amazing Journey.

Books, Ebooks, Audio Books and much more

www.creativekiwis.com

Bill Rosoman ebooks on Smashwords

http://www.smashwords.com/profile/view/leftfieldnz

Bill Rosoman books and ebooks on Lulu.com

http://stores.lulu.com/leftfieldnz

Bill Rosoman Amazon.com books/ebooks

http://goo.gl/MLSLL

Craig Lock Amazon.com books/ebooks
http://goo.gl/vTpjk

Craig Lock ebooks on Smashwords
https://www.smashwords.com/profile/view/craiglock

Craig Lock books and ebooks on Lulu.com
http://www.lulu.com/spotlight/craiglock

Creative Kiwis Videos at
www.youtube.com/leftfieldnz

Creative Kiwis Blog

http://leftfieldnz.wordpress.com/

Bill Rosoman Books/Ebooks

The Ultimate Desktop Publishing Book

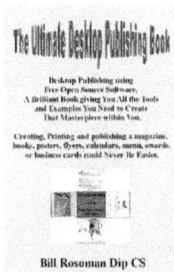 Desktop Publishing using Free Open Source

Software. A Brilliant Book giving You All the Tools and Examples You Need to Create That Masterpiece within You. Creating and publishing a magazine, books, posters, flyers, calendar, menu, award certificates, or business cards could Never Be Easier. Using Free Open Source Software FOSS. Scribus, Open Office, Gimp, Inkscape, Calibre. By Bill Rosoman Dip CS

http://www.lulu.com/product/paperback/the-ultimate-desktop-publishing-book/14847923

http://www.smashwords.com/books/view/49688

The Simple On The Road Cook Book

The Simple On The Road Cook Book. A Useful Easy, Simple and Budget Conscious Guide for Bachelors and other Food Preparation and Cooking Challenged People. Especially if Living in a Confined Space or On The Road.

http://www.lulu.com/content/paperback-book/the-simple-on-the-road-cook-book/8674457

Howto for Windows and Internet Virgins (book)

A Howto for Windows and Internet Virgins using the Windows Operating System. A Beginners Guide to using Window

http://www.lulu.com/content/paperback-book/howto-for-windows-and-internet-virgins/6121427

Te Ao Wiremu, Bill's World

Te Ao Wiremu, Bill's World, Honorary Black, Thirty years on the East Coast. Bill Rosoman spent 29 years living and working on the East Coast of the North Island of New Zealand above Gisborne. This is his yarn about his life there and the funny and not so funny things that happened.

http://www.lulu.com/content/paperback-book/te-ao-wiremu-bills-world/4030752

http://goo.gl/0v28l

Get a Life (The Dummies Guide To Life)

The book "Get a Life (The Dummies Guide To Life)", grew out of my brushes with life and my life long study of and fascination with human nature. I also had a bout of cancer in 2006. I find it interesting how people react to big events like finding out you have cancer. Personally I believe you have to take the good with the bad and get on with it. So I decided to write my thoughts down on my laptop and see what comes up! LOL The opinions expressed are mostly my own with help from quotations etc.

http://www.lulu.com/content/paperback-book/get-a-life-%28the-dummies-guide-to-life%29/1262704

http://www.smashwords.com/books/view/31925

Android Tablet Apads How to

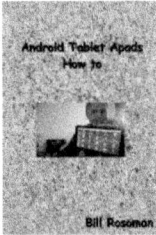

Android Tablets Apad How to", Some great Information for the use of Android Tablets. Tablets are the device of the future.

http://www.smashwords.com/books/view/35819

EPUB, How To Write and Publish an Ebook

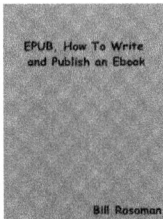

An ebook, "EPUB, How To Write and Publish an Ebook", using free software (FOSS), Writing and publishing and ebook is quite different from a hard copy book. This ebook gives you all the basic software and knowledge and skills to create your own epics for the modern age.

http://www.smashwords.com/books/view/32052

Puppy Linux Manual

An ebook, "Puppy Linux Manual", Some great Information for the use of Puppy Linux, a Free Operating System which is great on older computers. Puppy Linux is also good for formatting and partitioning hard drives and rescuing data from crash computers.

http://www.smashwords.com/books/view/35818

Bill's Tome

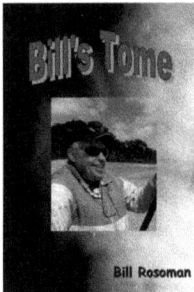

An ebook, "Bill's Tome", All That I Know Life, the Universe, Mortality etc.!

https://www.smashwords.com/books/view/41385

Creative Kiwis, an Amazing Journey

Creative Kiwis, an Amazing Journey

www.creativekiwis.com

Bill Rosoman and Craig Lock

An ebook, "Creative Kiwis, an Amazing Journey", this book is about the journey of two people in the world of the Internet and Ebook and Book Publishing and Marketing. A massive journey and learning process.

http://goo.gl/Q9ZJ3

http://www.smashwords.com/books/view/43270

A'holes That I've Known

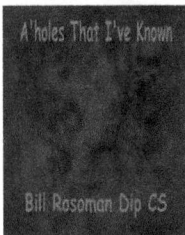

A look at some of the A'holes I have meet in my life. Life is not always a bed of roses and you have to deal with some not so nice people. Still life is great and you move through life and it's ups and downs. Being confident, articulate and assertive is the way to go, no door mouse for me. LOL

http://www.smashwords.com/books/view/44346

http://www.lulu.com/product/paperback/aholes-that-ive-known/14963987

Don't Say Can't

Don't Say Can't, an ebook about the bad habit of people saying can't, and how we should live in a "Can't Free Zone". Do you continue to bang your head against a brick wall and continually meet the same obstacles of life or do you stop saying can't and branch out in a new and positive direction in your life.

http://www.smashwords.com/books/view/55083

http://www.lulu.com/product/paperback/dont-say-cant/15822569

Way Outback

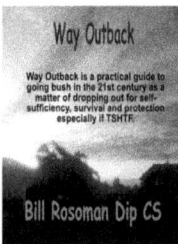

Way Outback is a practical guide to going bush way out back in the 21st century as a matter of dropping out financially for self-sufficiency, survival and protection, especially if TSHTF. People do not plan to fail, they just fail to plan.

http://www.amazon.com/dp/B006TJVE06

http://goo.gl/e79mB

http://www.lulu.com/product/ebook/way-outback/18813190

TOP

Craig Lock Books/Ebooks

A New Dawn

A passionate story of inspiration: hope, faith, peace and especially LOVE for the world and inspired by what I simply term God, the Creative Source of Life itself. That is my legacy to my beloved family...and the world. "But they that wait upon the Lord shall renew their strength, they shall mount up with wings as eagles; they shall run and not be weary; and they shall walk, and not faint." - Isiah 40:31

http://www.lulu.com/product/paperback/a-new-dawn/13399980
https://www.smashwords.com/books/view/42372

RETURN OF THE CHICKENS (e-book)

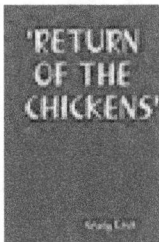

After that little interlude, I hope every one of you, the "New Safs" enjoy my book....and I hope you don't lynch me when you find me (like Salmon Rushdie) - something fishy going on? Because I believe that a sense of humour definitely helps in the hard but exciting years ahead of living in our "new beloved country".

http://www.lulu.com/content/e-book/return-of-the-chickens/9515900

Quote Unquote": Quotations that I like... very much (book)

This is one of my first manuscripts and a rather short one at that - just like the author. I have also included a separate section on motivational quotes for all salespeople and on business in general (see Part Two). These often helped me in my rather more formal previous commercial career. But even if you are not in business , nor in sales you might find them inspiring (or inspirational) as we journey through the game that is life. I do. ... so time to get right into it / them and get "cracking" or "weaving" as my dear mother would say.

http://www.lulu.com/content/paperback-book/quote-unquote
%e2%80%9d-quotations-that-i-like-very-much/9508150

Peace Lives Within (e-book)

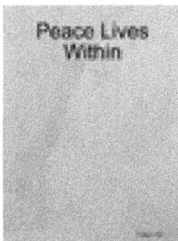

These are some notes that I've made recently (from my "red book"), which is forming the basis, the frame-work, the building-blocks for a new manuscript I'm writing. So will share with you and post extracts (hopefully regularly) on my Wordpress blog (craiglock.wordpress.com) as I write it. Hopefully I'll continue getting my "daily dose of inspiration".

https://www.smashwords.com/books/view/43299

http://www.lulu.com/content/e-book/peace-lives-within/9419604

To The End Of The Rainbow (e-book)

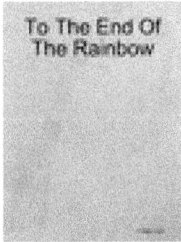

Craig has a 'passion' for writing books that tell stories about people doing positive things in this often so hard, sometimes unkind world, occasionally so cruel, yet always amazing world He loves 'telling tales', sharing true stories that leave the reader feeling uplifted, empowered and perhaps hopefully even inspired. Craig loves to try to "test his writing limits and imagination"and is currently writing 'To The End of the Rainbow'. I don't know how my story will end, but I do know how it all began!

http://www.lulu.com/content/e-book/to-the-end-of-the-rainbow/9419597

Angolan Dawn (book)

A true tale of an Angolan migrant miner who goes to 'e'Goli', the big city of gold in South Africa. Also a realistic portrayal of the Angolan conflict in "darkest Africa" through the eyes of a hospital orderly. A moving and realistic novel about the evil and destructiveness of war, as well as the inherent goodness within every human spirit. History, Angola, Southern Africa, Legacy, Gisborne, New Zealand, South Africa, Travel, Africa, War, Politics, Humanity, Conflict, Novel

http://www.lulu.com/content/paperback-book/angolan-dawn/8391177

How to Write a Book and Get Published (book)

Get Cracking and get your book written, completed and published now! We offer the complete package of helping you write that book within you and to get it published. At the end of the book you will have a published book, if you have a manuscript ready to go!

http://www.lulu.com/content/paperback-book/how-to-write-a-book-and-get-published/7313395

The New Rainbow (book)

THE NEW RAINBOW A tale of the many people in the rainbow nation of New South Africans http://www.lulu.com/content/paperback-book/the-new-rainbow/7074514

I'LL DO IT MY WAY (book)

Childhood in South Africa, South African Politics and Apartheid and our new life in New Zealand

http://www.lulu.com/content/paperback-book/ill-do-it-my-way/6121816

Handbook for Survival in the Nineties and especially the New Millennium (book)

A collection of writings on various subjects to help every man or woman survive in a rapidly changing, uncertain world... after the "easy living and prosperity" of the seventies and eighties. An introductory look at the concepts of success, motivation, attitude, goal setting and stress

https://www.smashwords.com/books/view/43289

http://www.lulu.com/content/paperback-book/handbook-for-survival-in-the-nineties-and-especially-the-new-millenium/1660924

The End of the Line (book)

This is Craig Lock's first novel. A short novel set in "the beloved country". A passionate and heart-breaking tale of South Africa, a true story of the bad old days, but with the hope of the new. "The End Of The Line" could be described as a "faction", a fiction with a serious factual grounding. It is simple, and therefore moving. It gives yet another highly individual portrait of that troubled land, and it does so through a believable and sustained narrative form."

http://www.lulu.com/content/paperback-book/the-end-of-the-line/1630869

https://www.smashwords.com/books/view/42710

Dropped out In Godzone (book)

A new immigrant's impressions of life in provincial New Zealand (after coming from a large city in South Africa) ... and there were one or two rather funny adventures, nay escapades in "Sleepy Hollow" from time to time.

http://www.lulu.com/content/paperback-book/the-end-of-the-line/1630869

https://www.smashwords.com/books/view/42699

Over The Rainbow (book)

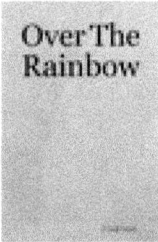

Over The Rainbow

A look at the many colourful peoples, who make up this diverse and vibrant society, as seen through the eyes of a newspaper reporter. Many colourful "vignettes" in this "land of great contrasts" - happy, sad and true, that was the fabric of South African life in the lead up to the historic Democratic Election of 1994. We live in a very complex country of great disparities and extremes, especially in wealth and in living standards. A land of great contradictions: a land of sunshine, a world in one country, a land of laughter in this strange and beautiful place. Much of the laughter from the very people, who have suffered the most and felt the most pain in this strange tormented place of ours. Yes, there is that sadness in the eyes of them too. So to put it simply, South Africa is just one happy, sad land...and I hope that the lives of ALL South Africans will become better in the days ahead.

http://www.lulu.com/content/paperback-book/over-the-rainbow/1265824

Here There and Everywhere

Craig Lock is an extensive world traveller and failed professional emigrater who has spent most of his life's savings on airfares. He is still 'sliding down the razor blade of life', stuck on a deserted (other than a few brilliant rugby players) island at the bottom of the world near Antarctica, where he is 'trying to throw a double six' to get off and go out into the real world - but he doesn't know where! In the style of Bill Bryson, HERE, THERE AND EVERYWHERE tells tales of His hilarious hair-raising adventures in his younger years through 'Grate' Britain and the Continent.

https://www.smashwords.com/books/view/44410

http://www.lulu.com/product/paperback/here-there-and-everywhere/15050656

Jochen Rindt World Champion F1 Driver

by Bill Rosoman

Jochen Rindt World Champion F1 Driver

Summary
Jochen Rindt, was a Super F1 driver.

IMHO Jochen Rindt is the best F1 Driver of all times

He Died and was awarded the F1 Trophy posthumously.

Motor Racing in the 1960s and 1970s was an exciting time and the sport was much different than it is today.

Jochen Rindt for me was the pinnicle of a super sportsman and a great person, who lived in times that were much simplier .

Keywords
F1, Jochen Rindt, Motor Racing, Car Racing, F1 Racing, Sport

###

www.ingramcontent.com/pod-product-compliance
Lightning Source LLC
Chambersburg PA
CBHW071802020426
42331CB00008B/2376